Stories in this book

Page

BIBLE ANIMALS
2018 Colin Tinsley
ISBN 978-1-909751-84-2

Published by

www.hopeforyouthministries.org
Colin Tinsley
6 Hawthorn Hill, Kinallen, Dromore,
Co. Down, BT25 2HY, Northern Ireland
Email hopeforyouthministries@gmail.com
Web www.hopeforyouthministries.org

1. The Talking Snake

Have you ever wondered where the world came from and how we got here? When we go back to the very beginning of the world, we come across the first man and woman, Adam and Eve.

God has always existed. He was never made, invented or created. God made this world and everything in it in just six days. He simply said, "Let there be..." and immediately it was there. God created the earth, the animals, the plants and trees, the sea and dry land, every bird and sea creature, the stars, sun, moon, galaxies, and everything in this world – both the things you can see and those you can't!

Then God made a man – but unlike everything else that He spoke into existence,

3

God used something to make him. The Bible tells us that God took some dust from the ground and created man. However, man was different to the animals

because God breathed into man and he became a living soul. Our souls are the part of us which connects us to God.

God wanted something to worship Him, so that is why He made human beings. Our ultimate purpose on earth is to worship God and enjoy Him forever. He desires to be part of our lives but He gives us freewill to decide if we want to involve Him in our lives. Animals, on the other hand, do not have a soul and therefore cannot enjoy the same relationship with God as we can.

God placed Adam and Eve in a garden called Eden. There they were put in charge of all the animals God had made. God gave them one rule to show their obedience to Him: they were not allowed to eat of a particular tree in the middle of the garden. This tree was called the Tree of the Knowledge of Good and Evil. If they disobeyed God and ate the fruit of the tree, then they would die and not live forever.

Meanwhile, in Heaven, there was a problem brewing. The most beautiful of all the angels – in fact, the chief angel, rebelled against God's authority. As a result, God cast him out of Heaven and from that moment, that angel became the devil and has opposed God ever since.

Tree of Knowledge

The devil entered a serpent (snake) in the Garden of Eden and slithered up to Eve. He asked her why she was not eating from the Tree of the Knowledge of Good and Evil in the middle of the garden. Eve told the snake that if she ate from the tree, then she would die. The snake laughed and deceived her by saying she had misunderstood God and if she ate from the tree, she would only become wise like God.

Eve believed the lie of the devil and disobeyed God by eating from the tree and offering the

fruit to Adam as well. Later that day, in the evening time, when God came walking in the garden, He called Adam and Eve by name. Once they heard God call them, they hid because they knew they had done wrong.

God found them and asked them why they had disobeyed Him. Adam blamed Eve and Eve blamed the snake (controlled by the devil). God told them that their disobedience had brought sin into the world and as He had previously told them, one day they would die. Worst of all, they had broken their intimate connection with God and were barred from entering the garden again. As a result of their actions, all their descendants have been born with a sinful nature. The Bible tells us that sin entered the world by one man and the only punishment for that sin was death. But the good news is that our sins can be forgiven because God sent his Son, Jesus Christ, to die on a cross and pay the penalty our sins deserved.

1. **What did God make when He created the world?**

2. **Why did the snake tempt Eve to disobey God?**

3. **When we are told not to do something, why do we often do it?**

4. **When we are tempted to do wrong, what should we do?**

PRAYER...

Dear Lord, thank You for creating this world so beautifully. You made the trees, mountains, rivers and all the animals. Most of all, You made me. So I want to say thank You from the bottom of my heart. Please help me when I am tempted to be strong enough to say 'no'. In Jesus' name, Amen.

READ IT IN THE BIBLE | GENESIS 3:1–15

2. The Ram that was Stuck

Abraham was an old man at one hundred years old and his wife, Sarah was ninety. Many years before, God had promised them both that He would give them a son. As the years passed by, they probably wondered when their son would be born.

One day, angels visited them and reminded them that they would definitely have a son. Sarah laughed at the thought of it realising she was much too old. The

angels asked Sarah why she laughed, but she denied doing so. Then about a year later, Sarah gave birth to a baby boy, who they called Isaac. They were naturally overjoyed with him and cherished him dearly.

Abraham was a wonderful man of God who loved the Lord with all his heart. However, Abraham soon began to spend much more time with Isaac than he did with God. It was as if he loved his son more than he loved God. God teaches us that we are to love Him more than anything, and anyone.

God then put Abraham to the test to see how much he loved Him. In Bible times, they would often sacrifice an animal as a sign that the peoples' sins would be forgiven. When Jesus died on the cross, the sacrifice of animals stopped because all the other sacrifices pointed to that ultimate one. One night God spoke to Abraham and asked him to prepare his son, Isaac, as a sacrifice. Abraham thought he misunderstood God and asked him if he had indeed said his son, Isaac. "Yes," God told him, "your son, Isaac."

Now Abraham was faced with the most difficult decision of his life. Was he going to obey what God asked him to do or ignore Him? Abraham thought long and hard. He loved his little son so much but he could not choose him over God. So early the next morning, he packed his bags and set off with Isaac and his donkeys, on a long, 50 mile journey to Mount Moriah.

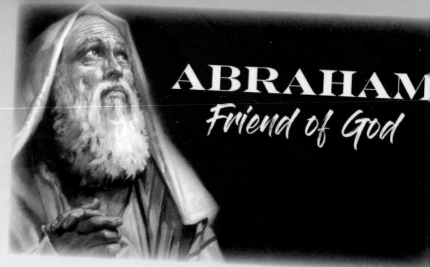

ABRAHAM
Friend of God

When they reached the bottom of the mountain, Abraham told his servants to wait there for him and Isaac to return after worshipping. Abraham's faith in God was so strong that he believed God would bring him back to life again. Abraham believed the promise God had made years earlier that he would be the father of a great nation and Isaac was part of that plan.

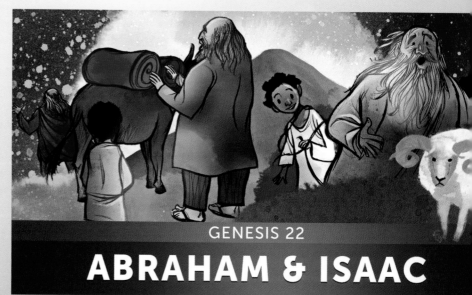

GENESIS 22
ABRAHAM & ISAAC

As they neared the top of the mountain, Isaac asked his dad where the animal was that would be sacrificed. Normally it was a sheep, goat or cow. Abraham looked at Isaac and gently told him that God would provide Himself with a sacrifice. He then sat Isaac down and explained how the Lord had asked him to offer Isaac as a sacrifice. This was a picture of what the Lord Jesus would do many years later on Mount Calvary, where He would be crucified for the sins of the world.

Isaac didn't run away, but willingly climbed on to the stones which formed the altar. Similarly, this was a shadow of how the Lord Jesus would willingly lay down His life for our sins. No doubt after telling Isaac how much he loved him, Abraham lifted his knife and stretched out his arm ready to slay his son. At that crucial moment, the angel of the Lord shouted "STOP! Don't lay your hand on Isaac – God didn't tell you to kill your son, but rather to offer him for a sacrifice!"

Abraham turned around and there, caught in a bush, was a ram (male sheep). He set Isaac free and the ram became a substitute

in Isaac's place. This draws another parallel with our salvation in Christ. Because of our sins, we deserve to die but Jesus became our substitute and took the punishment our sins deserved when He died on the cross. This was necessary to meet the demands of God's perfect justice so our sins could be forgiven. God provided Abraham with a ram because Jesus was the Lamb of God sacrificed for us.

1. **Why did God test Abraham?**

2. **What did God ask Abraham to do?**

3. **How does Isaac remind us of Jesus?**

4. **How does the ram remind us of Jesus?**

5. **What should we love more than anything else in the world?**

PRAYER...

Dear Lord, this might have been difficult for me to understand, but I have learned some new things today. I should always love You more than anything else in the world. I also learned that Jesus died on the cross for my sins so I don't have to be punished. Thank You so much for sending Your Son to do this for me. In Jesus' name, Amen.

READ IT IN THE BIBLE | GENESIS 22:1–14

3. The Thirsty Camels

This is a lovely, romantic story about a man finding a wife. Abraham had a son called Isaac, the little boy we read about in the last chapter. Just like God had promised Abraham a son, He also promised Isaac a son. However, by the age of 40 Isaac hadn't married and his father Abraham was concerned for him.

Subsequently, Abraham asked one of his servants to do him a favour and make a long journey to a faraway country to find a wife for Isaac. Abraham had distant relatives who lived there and he hoped they could help him find a wife for Isaac.

The servant took some other servants along with ten camels and started the long journey which took many days to complete. Finally, they reached the city which happened to have a well outside it where everyone came to draw their water. In those days they didn't have sinks and taps like we have today.

Abraham's servant then felt led to pray for wisdom and discernment. His prayer is one of the most wonderful prayers in the Bible. He asked the Lord to do something very unusual and specific. He told the Lord he would ask each woman who came to the well for a drink. If she offered him a drink that would be fine, but if she offered to draw water for his camels too, then he would take that as a sign that she was God's choice to be a wife for Isaac.

14

This was a very unusual prayer and an almost impossible task. A camel has nine stomachs to store water for long journeys – and the servant had ten camels! In effect, he was asking a stranger to carry the equivalent of ninety buckets of water! Who would do such a task for a complete stranger?

GENESIS 24

ISAAC & REBEKAH

Before he had even finished praying, a woman came walking towards the well to draw water. Without hesitating, the servant asked her for a drink of water. "Yes, of course," she said, "and do you mind if I draw water for your camels as well?" The servant probably was close to falling into the well with shock as he couldn't believe what he was hearing – his prayer had been answered immediately!

This woman was called Rebekah, but the servant never told her what he had been praying for or the reason he had come to her country. He asked to be introduced to her father and when she brought him to their house he told her father the whole story, including the prayer at the well and how Rebekah had offered to draw water for his thirsty camels.

Rebekah's father looked at her and asked if she would go with this man to marry Isaac. Rebekah chose to go. She was an adult after all and could make up her own mind but it was still a step of faith. This is what it is like to become a Christian. No one has ever seen God, yet He wants us to trust Him and give our lives to Him. He loves us and cares for us and wants to be our Heavenly Father. Just like Rebekah trusted that it was God's plan for her to go and marry Isaac.

Isn't this an amazing account of the Lord's goodness, showing how He can answer prayer? God provided a wife for Isaac and after some time she bore him two sons – twins called Jacob and Esau.

1. In what ways was this an unusual prayer?

2. Are there any prayers too hard for God to answer?

3. How does this story remind us of being a Christian?

4. How can we put our faith in God?

PRAYER...

Dear Lord, thank You for this wonderful story of the thirsty camels. I am amazed at how You answered this man's prayer. Surely no prayer is too hard for You to answer! I know nothing is impossible with You. Help me to believe that You will answer my prayers too and help me realise You are always there for me, especially when I need help. Thank You for sending us Your Son, Jesus Christ. Please strengthen my faith in You. In Jesus' name, Amen.

READ IT IN THE BIBLE — GENESIS 24:1—66

4. The Talking Donkey

Did you know that donkeys can talk? Well, at least one we read about in the Bible could. There are two animals mentioned in the Bible that spoke. One was the snake in the Garden of Eden and the other one was a donkey belonging to a man called Balaam.

When God's special people, the Israelites, were travelling from Egypt to their Promised Land, Balak, the King of Moab was afraid they might try to take over his city. Immediately, he contacted a prophet called Balaam and asked him to curse the people - hoping that might stop the Israelites passing through his land. Balaam sought God about the matter

NUMBERS 22

BALAAM'S DONKEY

and the next day he informed Balak's messengers it would be wrong to curse the people because they were the chosen people of God!

When Balak heard that Balaam had refused his request, he tried to tempt Balaam by offering him some money as a reward if he would carry out the king's request. Balaam still refused until the king offered

him so much money, he gave into temptation and saddled off into the night to curse the people of God.

Balaam thought no one but the king knew what he was going to do. That's why he made his way during the night so no one would see him. One thing, he

seemed to forget though, was that God had seen him. God sees everything we do and even knows everything we think about. He knew all about Balaam's wicked plan to curse the people of God.

As Balaam hurried along the road to meet Balak, the Lord send an angel down from Heaven to stand in the middle of the road. However, the angel - who had a sword in his hand - was invisible to Balaam but his donkey saw him and stopped in her tracks and turned into a field. Balaam was furious and began beating the donkey to force her back onto the road, but the stubborn donkey refused.

As Balaam's anger flared, he beat the poor donkey even harder. This time the donkey squashed Balaam's foot against a stone wall and Balaam

became so furious, he tried to beat the donkey to death! Suddenly, the donkey spoke and asked Balaam why he was beating her. He was so furious, he wasn't even shocked when the donkey spoke to him! The donkey went on to tell Balaam that she had been faithful to him all his life. She had always carried him wherever he had wanted to go and even carried heavy loads for him when required.

Suddenly, the Lord opened Balaam's eyes to see the angel standing in

front of them with his sword drawn. Balaam was shocked and realised if the donkey had taken one more step, he would have been killed for what he was planning to do.

Balaam fell on his knees immediately and repented for what he was doing. God forgave him and that day used the talking donkey to spare Balaam's life. These were God's people Balaam was going to curse and God was looking after them too by intervening in this situation.

Saved by a Donkey

1.　Why did the donkey talk in the story?

2.　What was Balaam going to do in the middle of the night?

3.　In what way did the Lord protect the people that night?

4.　Is it ever right to do wrong?

5.　What should we do if we are ever tempted to do wrong?

PRAYER...

Dear Lord, thank You for including the story of the talking donkey in the Bible. Thank You for protecting Your people that day by sending an angel. Please help me not to give into temptation when it comes my way. Help me to be strong enough to say no. In Jesus' name I pray, Amen

READ IT IN THE BIBLE | NUMBERS 22:1–39

5. David and the Sheep

The Bible contains many stories about sheep. The most famous one is Jesus' Parable of the Lost Sheep - telling how a shepherd left his 99 sheep

safe in the fold and searched all night long until he found the one that was lost.

n the Old Testament, David s renowned for being the hero who killed the giant, Goliath, and later became King of Israel. However, in his early days, David was a simple shepherd boy who tended to his father's sheep. One day when the great prophet Samuel arrived at David's family home to anoint the next king, David's father didn't even bother bringing David in

from the fields. He reckoned he was too young and couldn't possibly be regarded as 'king' material!

In the fields, David didn't only make sure the sheep had plenty of lush grass, but in times o danger, he protected them a. well. One day, a bear attacked the sheep and stole one of the lambs. David didn't run away in fear, but rather ran after the bear and wrestled it until he rescued the lamb and killed the bear so it wouldn't strike again

On another occasion, a lion was prowling around near the sheep, which startled them. As the sheep ran off, David ran towards the lion and fought it with his bare hands, until he killed it too!

In quieter moments, when the sheep were safe, David spent a lot of time playing his harp and praying to God. It was during those hours alone in the fields that God taught David patience and how to trust in Him as part of his preparation for leading the nation of Israel.

David also had an excellent slingshot because whenever a sheep wandered off, he

learned to fire a stone in front of it to startle it and make it return to the flock. It is believed that David knew every sheep by name and if any sheep got injured, he took care of it.

As a Christian today, David reminds us of God while the sheep remind us of how we can be as God's people. God is always there caring for us and protecting us from harm and danger. Then when we wander off, He gently brings us back again.

Often we want to run off because it seems exciting but there are dangers out there awaiting us – just like bears and lions sought to harm the sheep. We should listen to our parents when they tell us not to do something. They always know best and are trying their best to protect us, even if we don't agree with them.

1. How was David able to defeat a lion and a bear?

2. **Why did David not allow the sheep to wander away?**

3. In what ways does David remind us of God?

4. **How does God keep us safe?**

5. Just like David loved the sheep, how does God love us?

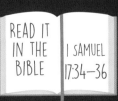

PRAYER...

Dear Lord, Thank You so much for looking after my family and me. Help me not to wander away from Your care, love and protection. Sometimes I want to do my own thing and go my own way, but help me to follow Your ways even if I don't fully understand them. I know You only want the best for me. In Your Son, Jesus' name, Amen.

READ IT IN THE BIBLE I SAMUEL 17:34—36

ELIJAH

The ravens brought him bread and meat in the morning, and bread and meat in the evening; and he drank from the brook.

I Kings 17:6

6. The Obedient Birds

This story is about a wicked king and queen. Their names were Ahab and Jezebel. They made a terrible law that people were no longer allowed to worship God. Instead they were told to worship a golden idol called Baal. God's prophet Elijah was appalled by this, so he visited King Ahab and told him that he and his friends only

worshipped the one true God of heaven and God tells us not to worship idols or any other gods. The king laughed at Elijah and told him he didn't need God anymore. He boasted that he was the king and could do anything he wanted. He told Elijah if he continued to worship God he would die.

Elijah

Elijah told the king he may be in control of the country, but he could not control the weather. Elijah prayed to God and asked Him to bring a drought on the land to show King Ahab who was really in control. God heard Elijah's prayer and it didn't rain for three and a half years! Very soon, the crops failed and the animals began to starve and eventually died.

God told Elijah to hide under a tree by a little brook called Cherith. There God protected Elijah and hid him from King Ahab for two years. God looked after His servant by giving him water from the little river and food from the sky! God spoke to birds called ravens – black birds that look like crows and told them to feed Elijah. Every day, the ravens brought him bread and meat and he never went hungry.

Isn't it amazing how these birds were so obedient to God's voice? Ravens are naturally scavengers who eat dead flesh and poke through rubbish, eating anything they can find. They also steal other birds' food as they can be very greedy and selfish. Yet, isn't it wonderful that out of all the beautiful and fascinating birds in the world like majestic eagles, God chose to use common ravens? God often chooses to use people or things

the world doesn't value. He can use anyone He pleases and He sees their real beauty.

The birds were willing to be used by God. They were obedient to His voice. It's not natural for a raven to share their food, but God helped them to share. God made the difference.

1.   Does God like it when we worship idols?

2.   Why did God stop the rain?

3.   How was Elijah fed every day?

4.   How were the ravens obedient to God?

5.   How can we be obedient to the Lord?

PRAYER...

Dear Father, this has been another fascinating lesson I have learned today. How You made those big raven birds bring food to Elijah, without them eating it on the way, amazes me. They were obedient, so please Lord, help me to be obedient to You as well. Help me also to be thankful for the food I have to eat and the water I have to drink to keep me alive. In Jesus' name I pray, Amen.

READ IT IN THE BIBLE | I KINGS 17:1–10

7. THE TWO BIG BEARS

Did you know that bears are mentioned in the Bible? When David was looking after sheep, a bear came and stole a lamb from the flock. David ran after the bear and wrestled with it to save the lamb.

In another story, we read about two bears chasing children in the forest. Why did they do that you might wonder?

ELISHA

In the Old Testament, God used prophets to pass on messages to the people. One of the people's most-loved prophets was called Elijah. Then, at the end of his ministry, God took Elijah straight to Heaven in a whirlwind, on a horse and chariot made of

fire. Elijah had earlier appointed Elisha as his successor and Elisha had witnessed Elijah's departure from the earth.

The people searched everywhere for Elijah but obviously couldn't find him anywhere! When Elisha explained how God had taken Elijah to heaven, they laughed at him and kept on looking for Elijah.

Sometime later, Elisha was walking through a forest and met a group of children and young people who were playing together. When they saw Elisha coming, they began to jeer, "Go up, you bald head!" They were mocking him because he had no hair and also because of what he had told the people about Elijah ascending into Heaven. He likely told them to stop mocking him but they continued to do so. Finally,

33

he told them if they didn't stop he would call bears out of the forest to chase them!

The children laughed at Elisha even more, until two big female bears appeared from the forest and attacked all 42 of them.

The story of the two big bears chasing the children who mocked Elisha quickly spread throughout all the nearby villages and people realised how serious it was to ridicule God's servant.

Sometimes we are told to stop doing something when we know it's wrong. That is the right time to stop. In this story, the children were warned to stop but they didn't listen or obey.

If anyone ever mocks or makes fun of you, be sure to tell them about the two big bears. God promises to look after and protect His children. When someone tells us they are a Christian, we should always respect them and remember that they are a child of God.

1. Why did the bears chase the children in the forest?

2. Why is it wrong to mock and make fun of someone?

3. What should we do if we are making fun of someone and they ask us to stop?

PRAYER...

Dear Lord, help me to never mock people or hurt them. Sometimes I might do it for fun but never let me harm someone by doing so. Thank You for the story of the bears. It reminds me not to make fun of people, especially Christians, because I know they are Your

READ IT IN THE BIBLE | 2 KINGS 2:23–24

8. The Lion Tamer

This story assures us how God is able to look after and protect His children. Daniel came face-to-face with hungry lions – the kings of the jungle – but they couldn't eat him because God didn't allow them to touch him.

The background is that Daniel and his three friends were brought to Babylon as slaves. They were specially chosen to be trained in the ways of the king because they were young and very intelligent. The king believed they needed to eat the meat on his table and drink his wine, but Daniel and his friends refused it. They knew God was the One who made them wise and it had nothing to do with the food they ate, although healthy food is important.

Then a law was made that on a specific day, everyone had to bow down and worship a golden statue which was an image of the king. God tells us not to bow down to any images, so Daniel's three friends refused to do so. As a result, they were thrown into a fiery furnace which was turned up seven times hotter than normal. When the king looked into the furnace at the three men, he asked, "How come there are four?"

The fourth one was the Lord Jesus Christ who stood with Daniel's three friends and protected them. The king commanded them to come out of the fire and the Bible

states that not even a hair on their bodies was singed and the smell of smoke wasn't upon them! The king's wise men were jealous of Daniel and his three friends. They made another law stating that no one was allowed to pray to God. Anyone who did would be thrown into a lions' den. Daniel loved to pray to God – in fact, he prayed three times every day – first thing in the morning when he woke up, then in the afternoon and finally in the evening before he went to bed.

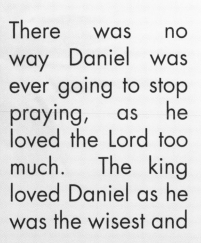

There was no way Daniel was ever going to stop praying, as he loved the Lord too much. The king loved Daniel as he was the wisest and

most trusted ruler who gave the king a lot of help. When the king's guards told him that Daniel had broken the new law and refused to stop praying, the king realised he had been tricked into signing it. The king had no choice but to watch Daniel be thrown into a den of hungry lions, which were fed people who disobeyed the king.

That night the king could not sleep. Early the next morning, he went down to look into the den to see what had happened to Daniel. He was amazed to see Daniel was still alive, sitting amongst the lions yet not one of them had harmed him! This had never happened to anyone before. God had protected Daniel and told the lions not to touch him. God is the great Lion-Tamer!

The relieved king released Daniel and commanded that the people who plotted against Daniel were thrown into the lions' den. Despite not touching Daniel for hours before, the Bible says the lions had gobbled these people up before they even touched the ground! The king then made a new law allowing people to freely worship Daniel's God.

1. In what ways did God protect Daniel and his friends in the story?

2. How can God look after us today?

3. In what ways was God important to Daniel?

4. What happened to the bad people who put Daniel into the lions' den?

5. Why is it important to pray to God?

PRAYER...

READ IT IN THE BIBLE | DANIEL :1–28

9. JONAH AND THE WHALE

In the Old Testament, we read about a man called Jonah. He was a prophet which means that God gave him messages to tell the people. In Bible times, there were no phones or modern technology and the Bible was in the process of being written. Hence, God had to communicate to people through prophets.

God told Jonah to visit a city called Nineveh. It was a huge city and the people who lived there were not interested in God. The Bible tells us that people were very wicked and God was angry because of the evil He saw there. It was so bad God would have to destroy the entire city before the evil spread across the world.

Salvation is of the LORD

Jonah 2:9

Despite their sin, God loved the people and really wanted

them to change their ways so He would not have to destroy the city. He told Jonah to warn them they had 40 days to repent otherwise they would have to face the consequences of their wrongdoing.

Jonah was afraid to go to Nineveh because he thought the people would be angry with him and chase him away. So he decided to board a boat travelling to Tarshish, which was in the opposite direction of Nineveh. He deliberately chose to disobey God and paid the fare, got on the ship and began to run away from God.

However, the Lord sent a great storm on the sea and soon the boat was swaying backwards and forwards in boisterous waves. The sailors were confused as to why the sea had changed so suddenly and they genuinely believed the boat was going to sink!

They started asking each other what they had done to make God angry, but one after another, they confessed they hadn't done anything wrong which may have caused the storm. Then they realised there was another passenger on the boat – Jonah, who was fast asleep in the hull. He thought he could hide from God and believed he could run away from Him.

"Wake up you sleeper, wake up!" the sailors roared at Jonah. "What have you done to make God so angry that He has made the sea so raging?" Jonah then began to tell his story about how God wanted him to go to Nineveh but he was so afraid he got on the boat

which was going in the opposite direction. Jonah said, "Throw me overboard and the sea will be calm." However, the sailors didn't want to do that, so they began to throw everything else overboard instead to try to make the ship lighter, but it made no difference.

Finally, they got Jonah by the hands and feet and threw him overboard. As soon as Jonah went into the sea there was a great calm. However, God hadn't finished with Jonah yet. The Bible says He prepared a great fish – likely a whale – to swallow up Jonah before he drowned. For three days and three nights, Jonah lived in the fish's belly.

During that time, Jonah began to pray and said sorry for running away from God. He promised God if his life was spared he would go to Nineveh and warn the people to repent of their sins or expect to face God's judgement. God heard Jonah's prayer and told the whale, to swim to Nineveh and spew Jonah up on the beach! It took Jonah three days to walk around the city, it was so big! When he preached and challenged the people to repent of their sins and

Salvation is of the LORD

Jonah 2:9

turn to God, they believed him and turned from their wicked ways. God acknowledged their genuine sorrow and His anger subsided.

After the 40 days, Jonah climbed up a hill outside the city to see what would happen. No destruction came and God didn't judge the city.

Meanwhile, Jonah seemed angry that God didn't execute judgement on Nineveh because he wanted God to punish them. God is so loving and forgiving that He loves and forgives people, even when others don't want Him to.

1. Why did Jonah run away from God?

2. What did God tell the big fish to do?

3. Why did God not destroy the city?

PRAYER...

Dear Lord, thank You for this story of Jonah. We are reminded how much You love us and care for us. Help me never to run away from You but rather run towards You every time I need help. In Jesus' name, Amen.

READ IT IN THE BIBLE — JONAH 2:1-10

10. Feeding the Pigs

Jesus told a parable about a father who had two sons. One day, the younger son asked his father if he would give him his inheritance immediately rather than waiting until his father's death. Although it was a somewhat rude request, his father agreed to give the younger son half of his wealth.

Once the younger son received the money, he packed his bags and left home to travel the world. He made his way to a faraway country, and there he wasted his money by living foolishly.

When you have plenty of money, it often attracts friends who are happy to help you spend it! However, when you spend money without receiving any more, it soon runs out.

This is what happened to the younger son's money – after some time it ran out, and then his friends ran off. They only wanted to be his friend when he had something to give them. Sadly they were not real friends.

Very soon this young man became hungry but he had no money left to buy food. He also wanted a comfortable bed to sleep in, but couldn't afford accommodation anywhere. He was desperate and realised he needed to find a job so he could earn some money.

The only job he was offered was looking after pigs and feeding them. As a Jewish man, this was a desperate situation as Jewish people don't eat pork. This is because the Old Testament law stated they were unclean animals. We have an indication as to how hungry he was because the Bible tells us he even wanted to eat the pigs' food!

As he sat there, he began to think about home. He realised life at home with his father was actually very good and he didn't appreciate how kind his father was to him. He always had enough food and a warm bed to sleep in at home. In fact, his father's hired servants even had comfortable beds, good food and spending money as well.

Finally, he came to his senses and swallowed his pride. He decided he would return to his father and ask him if he would make him like one of his hired servants, as that would be a lot better than living with pigs. So the next morning, he began the long journey back home again, no doubt wondering if his father would even look at him again!

However, the whole time his son had been away, his father never forgot about

him. It is likely that every morning he would gaze out the window waiting, hoping and expecting his son to come home. Suddenly one day, he couldn't believe his eyes as he saw his son in the distance! He was so excited he ran as fast as he could to meet his son. He hugged and kissed him, as he cried tears

of joy, delighted to have his son home.

As the son began to apologise and beg forgiveness, the father just hugged him and assured him all would be well. He ordered a robe for him to wear, shoes for his feet and a ring for his finger. He also arranged a big feast to celebrate and asked for the fattest calf to be killed and cooked to mark the safe return of his son.

"This, my son, was dead, and is alive again; he was lost, and is found." Jesus told everyone listening that in Heaven, it is the same when someone becomes a Christian. All the angels rejoice because someone who was lost has been found and one day will be in Heaven forever.

1. Why did he want the money and to leave a home where he was loved dearly?

2. What happens when you spend all your money foolishly?

3. What would it be like living with pigs?

4. How desperate must this man have been to eat the pigs' food?

5. When the father forgave him, how does that remind us of ourselves and God?

PRAYER...

Dear Father, You are such a forgiving God. Even though the man in the story forgot about his father, his father never forgot about him. Don't let me be a fool like the younger son in this story. He wasted all his money recklessly. Help me to be wise about my choices concerning friends and how I spend my money. Thank You for parents who love and care for me. In Jesus' name I pray, Amen.

| READ IT IN THE BIBLE | LUKE 15:11—32 |

11 The Fish with Pocket Money

When the Lord Jesus came to the town of Capernaum with His disciples, He was asked to pay some money - taxes of the city. He didn't have any money with Him and neither did His disciples. Rather than make excuses or cause a scene, he asked Peter, one of His disciples, if he would go and get some money.

The money was in a very unusual place. It wasn't in a house or hidden anywhere. He didn't borrow it from anyone or sell anything in exchange for money. Instead, Jesus told Peter to go to the harbour and cast a fishing line into the sea. There wasn't a magnet on the end of the line – it was just a normal fishing line. Jesus told Peter to pull the first fish he caught out of the sea and open its mouth.

Peter followed the Lord's instructions and within minutes, he caught a fish. When he reeled it in, he was amazed to find a coin in the fish's mouth! This was the exact amount needed to pay the tax in the city. God is so powerful, even the fish in the sea obey His voice! The fish picked up the coin on the seabed the moment God told it to.

Another time the disciples were out fishing together on the Sea of Galilee a few days after the Lord Jesus had died on the cross. Although they

were experienced fishermen, on this occasion they had fished all night in their boats but caught nothing. Early in the morning, the risen Jesus walked along the seashore and shouted over to them asking if they had caught anything.

When they replied "No", Jesus told them to cast their nets over to the

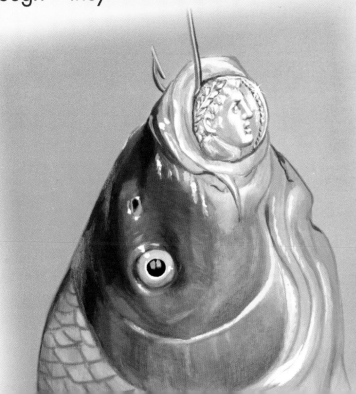

other side of the boat. They were probably insulted at such a remark but because it was the Lord, they obeyed Him, though possibly muttering under their breath, "How will this change anything?"

To their amazement, their nets were so full of fish, they had to call neighbouring

boats over to help them as their boat almost sank! While the disciples made their way to the shore, the Lord Jesus lit a fire and cooked some fish for them on the beach. He told them that even though they were fishermen by trade, from that moment on they were to be fishers of men. He wanted the disciples to tell everyone that He had rose from the dead so people could be saved by trusting and believing in Him.

1. How could the fish hear God when He told it to pick up a coin?

2. What were you thinking when you read how the nets were quickly filled with fish?

3. In what ways can you be obedient to God?

4. In what ways can God speak to us like He spoke to the fish?

5. How can we be fishers of men?

PRAYER...

ear Lord, I am so amazed at Your power, how even the fish can hear You speak to them.
elp me to be a fisher of men and tell all my friends how wonderful You are. Sometimes
hey might not want to know about You, but help me to tell them anyway. In Jesus' name.

READ IT IN THE BIBLE | MATTHEW 17:21—27

12. THE LITTLE DONKEY

The time had finally come for the Lord Jesus to walk through the streets of Jerusalem. It was Palm Sunday, a few days before Jesus was crucified on the cross.

Jesus didn't just walk through the streets of Jerusalem – He chose to ride a little donkey. The donkey wasn't specially trained or owned by a king. Rather, the Bible says it was a colt (young donkey) that no one had ever sat on before.

When the disciples brought the little donkey to the Lord Jesus and He sat on it, it

didn't buck Him off. This is unusual because unless a donkey is trained, it will naturally buck people off.

However, when Jesus sat on the donkey it became tame and He took immediate control of it. Although it is wild by nature, Jesus calmed it instantly!

This is what God does to people when He saves them and takes control of them. He does this by giving them power to overcome their sin, anger, frustration and jealousy and the person becomes a new creation. They don't change on the outside, but inside their

desires and character will change. Just like Jesus tamed the little donkey, He can help us control our behaviour and become more like Him.

It is interesting that Jesus chose to ride a little donkey. He could easily have chosen a striking black stallion, a lion or an elephant, yet He chose an insignificant little donkey to bring Him to the people.

Why did Jesus do this? Was it because He was humble, despite being the King of kings and the Saviour of the world? God doesn't view greatness as the world does. Fame, strength, good looks or intelligence isn't important to Him. God loves to use ordinary people!

Do you realise that you can be like the donkey in the story? It was used to bring Jesus to the people. That's what we have to do – bring the Good News of Jesus to people. One way we can do this is by telling all our friends what a wonderful person Jesus Christ is and how He has changed our lives.

Everyone was delighted to see Jesus that day. They took off their coats and waved palm branches shouting, "Hosanna! Hosanna!" However, Jesus knew that just a few days later, the same people would be crying and shouting, "Away with Him! Crucify Him! Crucify Him!" But the little donkey kept walking and fulfilled its job of bringing Jesus to the people.

1. **Why was Jesus going to Jerusalem?**

2. **In what ways can we be like the little donkey?**

3. **Why did the donkey not buck Jesus off?**

4. **Why did Jesus choose to use a little donkey?**

5. **How can the Lord Jesus take control of us?**

PRAYER...

Dear Lord, thank You for using the little donkey. You could have used a big horse or an elephant, but You chose to use a donkey. I know You are interested in ordinary people like me. Please use me and help me to understand Your plan for my life. Help me also to tell my friends about the little donkey because it took You to Jerusalem where You died for people like me. Thank You so much. In Jesus' name, Amen.

READ IT IN THE BIBLE | MATTHEW 12:12–16

Do you recognise all these animals that are found in the Bible?